SAINT LUCY

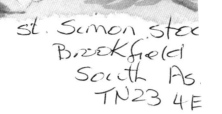

CTS Children's Books

CONTENTS

IN SYRACUSE

After his resurrection, Jesus appeared to the apostles and stayed with them for some days until it was time for him to go up to heaven.

Jesus said to his friends: "Go and announce the Gospel! Bring the Good News to all peoples and baptise them in the name of the Father and of the Son and of the Holy Spirit. Behold I am with you always, even to the end of time!" The apostles set out and went from city to city, travelling by land and by sea telling everyone about the love of God. This is how the Gospel reached Syracuse, a city on the island of Sicily. St Paul stopped there on his final journey and very soon a community of many Christians was formed.

Unfortunately being a Christian was against the law of the Roman empire and became ever more risky…

A GIRL IS BORN

In the third century after Jesus' birth, Sicily was a province of the Roman Empire. Syracuse was a splendid city by the sea and a lady called Eutychia and her husband lived there. They were of noble birth and were important people. They had a beautiful house and lots of servants.

Their house was decorated with paintings and statues and they had a courtyard surrounded by tall columns with a beautiful fountain in the middle, and plants and flowers all around.

In that house, around the year 280AD a beautiful baby girl was born. Her parents decided to call her Lucy which means 'light', perhaps because she was born at dawn or maybe to remind them that Jesus is the light of the world.

LUCY GROWS UP

Lucy's father died when she was very young. And her mother Eutychia brought Lucy up on her own, giving the little girl all her love. Lucy was educated like every daughter from a noble family and learnt many things from her teachers.

Eutychia took care of her and made sure that she knew about Jesus and his message of love.

As soon as she could understand, Eutychia told Lucy about Jesus, the son of God who came to live among men and she told her of his preaching, his parables and the miracles he worked and all the things he taught us. Eutychia also told her how Jesus was condemned to die on a cross even though he had done nothing wrong. Jesus didn't defend himself against the evil that was done to him but gave up his life for all of us. For this God did not leave him in death but raised him to life after three days.

Jesus opened the gates of heaven and gave us all the hope of the resurrection.

Lucy was a clever girl and listened carefully to her mother and asked her lots of questions. In a short time she knew all the stories about Jesus and about the first martyrs as well, all the men and women who had witnessed to their faith in Jesus to the point of dying for him. She was so struck by these words that in her heart Lucy decided to consecrate herself to Jesus, to be one with him like a bride is with her husband.

LUCY'S ENGAGEMENT

Lucy grew up quickly and became ever prettier, until one day a young nobleman from the city came to Eutychia and asked to marry her daughter. The young man was not a Christian but Eutychia liked him all the same. So not knowing about the decision that Lucy had taken in the secret of her heart she agreed to the engagement.

Eutychia also knew that she did not have long to live and wanted to make sure that Lucy would be well looked after when she died. If she married a rich young man she felt certain that Lucy would be alright.

Lucy didn't want to disappoint her mother so she accepted the young man's proposal. They celebrated the engagement soon afterwards; Lucy received a ring which was supposed to be the sign of the bond that joined them together… but in her heart she wanted something else.

THE PILGRIMAGE

Not long after, Eutychia became ill. Lucy was worried because her mother's illness was getting worse, so she thought of taking her to the tomb of St Agatha in the nearby city of Catania. Agatha was a young girl who had died as a martyr in 251AD when the emperor Decius had ordered a persecution of Christians in the empire. Agatha

preferred to give up her life rather than deny her faith in Jesus. Many people went to her tomb to pray and to receive the Holy Eucharist there and Lucy was sure that this would help her mother Eutychia as well.

Eutychia enthusiastically accepted her daughter's invitation and set off full of hope. In 301AD Eutychia and Lucy left on the pilgrim journey to Catania.

They arrived on the feast day of St Agatha which was the 5th of February. They heard the priest read the Gospel story of the sick woman who in the middle of a great crowd reached out to touch the hem of Jesus' cloak with the certainty that she would be cured.

So Lucy said to her mother: "Why don't you try to reach out and touch the tomb of St Agatha: you will see that St Agatha will ask Jesus to help you and that your prayer will be answered!"

Eutychia approached the tomb and touched it, and just like the woman in the Gospel she knew that Jesus had healed her. Both mother and daughter thanked God for his great gift!

Lucy's thoughts returned to the promise she had made in her heart to give herself only to Jesus and she also felt the desire to give all her money to the poor.

LUCY LOVED THE POOR

When they got home Lucy told her mother that she wanted to consecrate herself to Jesus and to sell everything she owned and to give it to the poor. In particular she wanted to give away all her dowry, all the money and things that her mother had collected and bought for her wedding. Lucy had given herself to Jesus and wanted to use her dowry for the poor whom Jesus himself taught are our brothers and sisters.

Eutychia at first refused because she feared for her daughter's future, but as time went on she saw how much Lucy wanted this and so she gave her permission and entrusted her daughter's decision to God.

Very soon, many poor people began to arrive at the posh house where Lucy and Eutychia lived. Lucy and her mother gave to everyone who asked and were a shining example of Christian charity. However, not everyone looked favourably on what Christians like Lucy and Eutychia were doing… The Roman Empire considered that the Christians were dangerous and in the years 303 and 304 the emperor Diocletian issued four edicts against them.

In these edicts were orders to destroy churches, burn the books of Sacred Scripture, imprison the leaders of the Christian communities and to force ordinary Christians to offer sacrifices to pagan gods. Those who refused were condemned to death.

THE TRIAL

The young man to whom Lucy was engaged had heard rumours of what was happening in Lucy and Eutychia's house so he went to see it with his own eyes. Lucy had to tell him the truth: "I can't marry you because I have given my heart completely to my Lord Jesus."

Hearing these words he went away full of anger and decided to go straight over to tell Paschasius the Roman Prefect, who was following the orders received from the emperor Diocletian and hunting down the Christians in Syracuse. So Eutychia and Lucy were arrested.

Lucy was brought before Paschasius who began to question her.

"Are you a Christian?"
he asked her.
Lucy answered:
"Yes, I am a Christian."
The prefect went on:
"Do you not know of the
order of our emperor Diocletian
that all Roman subjects must
sacrifice to the pagan gods?"

Lucy refused to offer
sacrifice to the pagan gods
and said:

"The only sacrifice that MY
God wants is love! My sacrifice
is to look after the poor: in these

past years I have given them all my wealth and now I am ready to give
my own self to my Lord."

LUCY REMAINED FAITHFUL

The prefect Paschasius tried in every way to convince Lucy to offer a sacrifice to the gods: that would have been a sign that she had given up her Christian faith. Lucy continued to refuse, and seeing that he was getting nowhere, Paschasius decided to have Lucy taken to the worst parts of the city and left there to be abused and dishonoured by the bad men who lived there.

The soldiers arrived and tried to take Lucy away, but no matter how hard they tried they could not move her.

Many more arrived and tried to push and pull her this way and that, but God would not allow anyone to take her away.

Paschasius did not know the power of the Spirit of God and thought that Lucy was being protected by magic, so he ordered that she be treated like a witch.

They prepared a fire to burn her at the stake in front of everyone. In an instant everything was prepared and the wood was placed around Lucy and oil poured over it. When the fire was lit, everyone was amazed to see that the huge flames were unable to touch Lucy.

Paschasius was furious and he ordered that the girl be killed immediately. A soldier obeyed his order, took his dagger and killed Lucy with it.

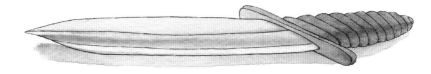

LUCY THE FRIEND OF JESUS

During her lifetime Lucy had followed the teachings of Jesus even if it meant going against her mother, against the wishes of her fiancé and even against the will of the emperor himself.

Lucy was brave and faithful, generous and full of hope, she was killed on the 13th December 304. In heaven Jesus, her teacher and friend, was waiting for her with a magnificent crown to place on her head.

Love is always stronger than evil and whoever bears witness to this is a light that wins even against the deepest darkness.

WAITING FOR ST LUCY

The 13th December is the feast of St Lucy. The place where they celebrate it most is of course the city of Syracuse where she was born. There they have a solemn procession where a silver statue of the saint is carried through the city. In Palermo they eat special food to remember St Lucy's help during a famine.

In Venice the feast is also celebrated because her body is said to be there. In Austria and the Czech Republic on the evening before her feast day, all the children wait for St Lucy to bring them gifts. In Denmark and Sweden they celebrate her feast by choosing a girl to dress like St Lucy and together with other girls they go and give gifts to poor children. All the girls dress in white and wear crowns with seven lighted candles on their heads.

ST LUCY'S LAMP

Lucy is a beautiful name and comes from the Latin word for light, which was the first thing that God created. Jesus also spoke of the light in the Gospel, he said: "I am the light of the world; whoever believes in me will not walk in darkness, but will have the light of life." (John 8:12)

In another passage Jesus said to his disciples:

"You are the light of the world; a city on a hilltop cannot remain hidden, nor is a lamp lit to be put under a tub, rather it is put on a lamp stand so that it gives light to everyone in the house. In the same way let your light shine in the sight of men, so that they see your good works and give glory to your Father who is in heaven." (Matthew 5:14-16)

With these words Jesus teaches us that if we follow his word we can bring the light of love to all those around us.

Many traditions surrounding St Lucy are to do with light. For her feast you could prepare a lamp either to keep in your house or to give as a present!

Take some modelling clay and roll it into a ball. Then press it down until it becomes flat and roughly triangular in shape.

Pinch the narrower end together to form a shape a bit like a spout.

At the other end take a smaller ball of modelling clay and press it onto the rest of the lamp in order to make a handle. Make sure you press it well so that the handle doesn't come off the lamp after it dries.

Take a candle and use it to make a hollow in the narrow end of your lamp. Then with a pencil press some decorations into the clay as shown. You can make some little stars.

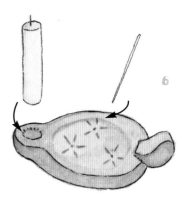

Allow the lamp to dry and then paint some glue onto the stars and sprinkle some glitter onto the glue.

Place the candle in the hollow and prepare a label to attach to the handle. You can write:

"You are the light of the world"

PRAYER

O Lord

You created light to dispel the darkness,

And have shone your light on all of creation;

You gave Jesus to the world

Who is a light for all mankind.

We pray that with your help

We can be like St Lucy

And reflect the light of your son,

His wisdom and hope,

And the light of His friendship and love.

Text by Silvia Vecchini
Illustrations by Antonio Vincenti
Translated by Pierpaolo Finaldi

Saint Lucy: Published 2009 by the Incorporated Catholic Truth Society, 40-46 Harleyford Road, London SE11 5AY. Tel: 020 7640 0042; Fax: 020 7640 0046; www.cts-online.org.uk. Copyright © 2009 The Incorporated Catholic Truth Society in this English-language edition.

ISBN: 978 1 86082 564 4   CTS Code CH 19

Translated from the original Italian Edition **Santa Lucia** - ISBN 88-87324-76-X, published by Il Pozzo di Giacobbe, Corso Vittorio Emanuele 32/34, 91100 Trapani (TP), Italy © 2005 Crispino di Girolamo.